Jesus Christ

FOREVER

*Inspirational Poetry
To Live By*

Betty H. Caldwell

Introduction

No matter how old you are, God can use you. Sometimes we convince ourselves that we are too old to take on new challenges, even if they mean furthering the Kingdom of God. During my lifetime, I have always focused on God, family, and my career.

Although I am now retired, I seem to be busier than ever. I love painting wildlife, landscapes, and other subjects dear to my heart; gardening, and providing homes to stray animals. In prior years, I taught Sunday school, worked as church secretary, and sang in church choirs. Although, in the recesses of my mind, I always felt that I should do more for my Lord.

Two years earlier, some very dear friends of ours had lost their only daughter to liver failure. My husband had the honor of officiating at her funeral. They then requested that he speak at a memorial service on the two-year anniversary of her death. As I thought about her passing and the upcoming memorial service, I wanted to share some comforting words to her family and friends. As I sat on our deck overlooking the flowers that were blooming so beautifully in our backyard, I realized the similarities the flowers had with the death of a loved one. The flowers die in the fall and then bound into resurrection the following spring. Our loved ones pass from this life but then will resurrect the day that Jesus returns.

With these thoughts in mind, I went to my computer and wrote "God's Flowers." I thought it was a one-time gift from God–but the Lord is still giving me poems to write. I will continue as long as it is His Will. My prayer is that these poems will point the way to Jesus and bring comfort to all who read them.

Dedications

The Lord Jesus Christ

It was His Grace and inspiration that enabled me to write these poems. It is my prayer that these poems will touch lives and help win souls for His Kingdom.

Mrs. Ruth M. Hagerman

My mother – a woman who deeply loves the Lord, her family, songbirds, and flowers. She has sacrificed so much in her life for her children. Her legacy will be her unconditional love for each of us. May God richly bless you, mom.

Reverend C. K. Caldwell

My husband of 52 years who has always been my encourager (my Barnabas) in all my life endeavors. His patience and love have always carried me through the times when I needed them the most. A man who truly loves the Lord and his family.

A Special Gift

The giving of a book to a friend is very special and meaningful. It sometimes allows the reader an insight into the soul of the giver. A good book will impart warm memories into a friendship with the reading of each page.

Please read and meditate on each poem. I pray the blessings you receive will be as great as those I received as I was writing them.

May God bless and keep you always.

— Betty H. Caldwell

Table of Contents

Blessings

Encouragement

Friendship

Grief

Hope

Love

Peace

Praise

Prayer

Protection

Salvation

Thankfulness

Trusting

Blessings

In the wee hours of the morning,
As wispy clouds drift by,
The moon is on its way to bed,
As daybreak comes alive.

The sun is quickly waking up,
To start a brand new day,
The birds are chirping in the trees,
As I begin to pray.

I told the Lord I loved Him,
How much He meant to me,
I thanked Him for His blessings,
And prayed for you and me.

I asked Him to protect you,
And bless you from above,
To hold you close next to His breast,
And shelter you with love.

Author: Betty H. Caldwell

Psalm 145: 18 "The Lord is nigh unto all them that call upon him, to all that call upon him in truth."

Cast Your Bread

Cast your bread upon the waters,
As the Bible tells you to,
If you adhere to what God says,
It'll come right back to you.

It's always better for us to give,
Then to receive, God said,
So let the things you think you love,
Bless someone else instead.

He'll open up His windows,
Pour blessings out on you,
You won't have room to store them,
Believe, for this is true.

Don't worry that you'll suffer,
Have needs that won't be met,
He'll see that you are safe and warm,
Just trust, He'll not forget.

Author: Betty H. Caldwell

Ecclesiastes 11:1 "Cast thy bread upon the waters: for thou shall find it after many days."

Heavenly Gifts

The Lord saw fit one day to give,
An earthly gift to me,
He blessed me with a husband,
Perfection, I could see.

As time went on, I then could see,
He was an earthly man,
He had some faults and weaknesses,
But God still had a plan.

God molded him and changed him,
He's now complete for me,
He loves the Lord and Savior,
And prays on bended knee.

God blessed me once again, no doubt,
With sons, my life's complete,
We taught them to obey His Word,
And prayed that His, they'd be.

Author: Betty H. Caldwell

James 1: 17 "Every good gift and every perfect gift is from above,
and cometh down from the Father of lights . . . "

19

His Wisdom

We think we have an answer,
On this old troubled Earth,
To all of mankind's troubles,
We don't need Jesus' birth.

It all was just a story,
A pipedream, someone said,
The God we knew no longer lives,
So, wake up, don't be led.

God smiles above and winks His eye,
He knows we'll learn a lesson,
He lets us make a few mistakes,
But He'll withhold His blessing.

He knew when He made Adam,
Free choice to him, He gave,
God wanted Adam's fellowship,
But Adam chose the snake.

Author: Betty H. Caldwell

Proverbs 1:7 "The fear of the Lord is the beginning of knowledge: but fools despise wisdom and instruction."

His Words

I never thought the day would come,
To write a Godly rhyme,
But then one day, the Lord inspired,
My heart to take the time.

I said, Dear Lord, You'll have to help,
Me with this chore of mine,
Just put Your Words into my head,
And then we'll make a rhyme.

I wrote the first one for my friends,
And thought that's all I have,
It's just a "one-time" gift to me,
Then, wrote one for my dad.

It seems they just keep coming,
The Lord keeps blessing me,
With words to keep on writing,
That bless the Trinity.

Author: Betty H. Caldwell

Ephesians 4:8 "Wherefore he saith, when he ascended up on high, he led captivity captive, and gave gifts unto men."

Little Children

Jesus blessed the little ones,
And said, bring them to me,
He taught that we should be like them,
If we should heaven see.

God said that they should honor,
Their parents in every way,
And they would have a longer life,
If they would just obey.

Like little children, we must be,
To enter in His gate,
Pure of heart and loving,
With humble, caring ways.

So don't be high and mighty,
And think it's up to you,
For pride will be your downfall,
The Lord will humble you.

Author: Betty H. Caldwell

Mark 10:14 "... Suffer the little children to come unto me, and forbid
them not: for of such is the kingdom of God."

Merciful Father

They wandered in the wilderness,
In a solitary way,
They found no place to rest for long,
No home to dwell and stay.

So hungry and so thirsty,
Their souls were in dismay,
They cried unto the Lord,
He helped them right away.

We, too, are like the Israelites,
We live our lives "our" way,
But then when things go very wrong,
We call on God and pray.

And God in His great mercy,
Will pick us up again,
We miss a lot of blessings,
When we don't live for Him.

Author: Betty H. Caldwell

2 Timothy 3:5 "Having a form of godliness, but denying the power thereof: from such turn away."

23

The Joy of Birds

Whenever I'm away from home,
I miss the simple things,
Like flowers blooming, neighbors, friends,
And all the birds that sing.

The little birds all wait for me,
They think that they are mine,
They sing and sit up in the trees,
And wait for dinner time.

My home down here is not eternal,
God gave it for a season,
He lent the birds and flowers too,
He knew they would be pleasing.

I'll care for these until He comes,
To take me safely home,
There must be birds in Heaven,
That grace Him with their songs.

Author: Betty H. Caldwell

Psalm 104:12 "By them shall the fowls of the heaven have their habitation, which sing among the branches."

The Rose

A little rosebud grew one day,
In a pretty flower bed,
Dew fell upon its pretty face,
And wet its little head.

It then became a blossom,
Its beauty was untold,
It lifted up its pretty face,
And then began to glow.

A child was passing by one day,
And said it's like no other,
She smiled and bent to kiss it,
And picked it for her mother.

God gives us pretty roses,
To care for and to love,
They're just a tiny blessing,
From our Savior up above.

Author: Betty H. Caldwell

Psalm 37:4 "Delight thyself also in the Lord; and he shall give thee the desires of thine heart."

Victory

The rain is softly falling,
And dawn is now in view,
The leaves of fall are changing,
From green to golden hues.

There is a certain peace it brings,
A calmness to my soul,
It makes me realize each day,
The blessings that I hold.

I have a loving family,
A God that loves me too,
Without Him, I'd be nothing,
His love is always true.

He loved enough to die for me,
How could that ever be?
I'll love my Lord forever,
He gave me victory.

Author: Betty H. Caldwell

1 Corinthians 15:57 "But thanks be to God, which giveth us the victory through our Lord Jesus Christ."

An Anchor

A ship may have smooth sailing,
With blue skies up above,
No winds or storms to harm us,
Just peace, and joy, and love.

But soon a storm is coming,
With thrashing waves and wind,
If we don't have an anchor,
Our ship won't sail again.

Life is like a ship at sea,
With storms that come and pass,
So we must have an anchor,
Or we may never last.

So always let our Savior,
Be Master of your ship,
He'll help you tread the water,
And never let you slip.

Author: Betty H. Caldwell

Hebrews 6: 19 "Which hope we have as an anchor of the soul, both sure and steadfast, and which entereth into that within the veil; . . . "

Believe

The whisper of the wind,
The cooing of the dove,
The daisy in the meadow,
All speak of His great love.

And as I look around me,
The mountains and the seas,
Sometimes, I feel so very small,
How could one not believe?

Some may say, there is no God,
But one day they will see,
His glorious coming from above,
And from Him, they will flee.

So we must try to reach them,
And teach them He's the way,
It's up to us to pray each day,
Their souls for Him to save.

Author: Betty H. Caldwell

Matthew 21:22 "And all things, whatsoever ye shall ask in prayer, believing, ye shall receive."

Don't Give Up

Lord, I'm feeling low today,
I pray, You'll help me see,
That when the world is caving in,
You'll always stand by me.

Don't let me be discouraged,
Just help me with my pride,
I'll try to find humility,
With You, Lord, by my side.

I pray each day as I should do,
Your Word, I read it too,
But Satan seems to creep right in,
To make me weak, it's true.

But Lord, I know Your power,
Will strengthen me each day,
No other can compare to You,
You're in my life to stay.

Author: Betty H. Caldwell

Psalm 119:114 "Thou art my hiding place and my shield: I hope in thy word."

Forgiving Yourself

In life, we all have had a day,
We'd just as soon forget,
But God has put them in the past,
So leave behind regret.

He made your life brand new again,
The day you met the Lord,
And put new thoughts inside your head,
On you, His love, He poured.

So please don't be discouraged,
If you should slip and fall,
Repent and He will pick you up,
He'll be there when you call.

He is a loving Savior,
But, he will judge you too,
Just live for Him with all your might,
And He will strengthen you.

Author: Betty H. Caldwell

1 John 1:9 "If we confess our sins, he is faithful and just to forgive our sins, and to cleanse us from all unrighteousness."

He Reigns

We hear so much sad news today,
It's hard to understand,
It seems the violence never ends,
It's spread throughout the land.

God told us it would be this way,
But faithful, we must be,
We must hold fast to Jesus,
Until His Face we see.

So, please don't be discouraged,
Just hold His Hand and pray,
He'll keep you through eternity,
No matter what they say.

He is the reigning Savior,
His kingdom's still the same,
Just wait and trust until that day,
Because we know He reigns.

Author: Betty H. Caldwell

Isaiah 60: 18 "Violence shall no more be heard in thy land, wasting nor destruction within thy borders; but thou shalt call thy walls Salvation, and thy gates Praise."

Keep Shining

This world is quickly spinning,
Some say, "out of control,"
Although it seems to be that way,
We know God has a goal.

So please don't be discouraged,
You know you're in His Hands,
He'll keep you and protect you,
In spite of worldly plans.

Sin started back with Adam,
When Satan slithered in,
And brought deceit into the world,
He thought that he would win.

But God had other plans, you see,
He knew about the cross,
He made a way to cleanse our sins,
And it was Satan's loss.

Author: Betty H. Caldwell

1 John 3:8 "He that committeth sin is of the devil; for the devil sinneth from the beginning. For this purpose the Son of God was manifested, . . . "

Master of the Sea

Life is like uncharted seas,
Where we are tossed about,
We may have no direction,
Be full of fear and doubt.

The storms keep getting bigger,
The winds will not abate,
Our life is feeling hopeless,
For help, we cannot wait.

The storms will give us strength,
As we sail the raging sea,
As long as Jesus is our guide,
His harbor, we shall see.

So let the Master of the seas,
Become your guiding light,
He'll guide you safely home again,
Before the coming night.

Author: Betty H. Caldwell

Luke 8:24 ". . . Then he arose, and rebuked the wind and the raging of the water: and they ceased, and there was a calm."

My Redeemer

He saw the sin of man one day,
And said this cannot last,
Although ol' Satan laughs at Him,
He'll soon be in the past.

For evil will not triumph,
His Word is true, I know,
He will destroy him one day,
Because He told me so.

So child of God, don't worry,
We're on the winning side,
Obey His Word and trust Him,
And in our Lord, abide.

You'll see Him in the Eastern sky,
In Glory, He will shine,
We'll see Him then, just as He is,
And this Redeemer's mine.

Author: Betty H. Caldwell

Revelation 20:10 "And the devil that deceived them was cast into the lake of fire and brimstone, where the beast and the false prophet are . . ."

Our Comforter

When Jesus Christ ascended,
To His Father up above,
He left us with The Comforter,
To guide our lives with love.

The Comforter will dwell in us,
And help us understand,
The things that Jesus said to them,
When walking here with man.

He brings sweet peace from Jesus,
The world cannot command,
Don't let your heart be troubled,
Don't be afraid of man.

He'll stay with us 'til Jesus comes,
To take His Bride away,
So, don't you be discouraged,
Just live for Christ each day.

Author: Betty H. Caldwell

John 15:26 "But when the Comforter is come, whom I will send unto you from the Father, even the Spirit of truth, which proceedeth from the Father . . ."

Storms

Some days it seems that all goes wrong,
And nothing works out right,
I struggle hard to make it through,
And then I realize.

That God sends rain upon us all,
I think a cloud is stuck,
It's hanging on my head, it seems,
I need a change of luck.

But, hold on just a minute,
I don't believe in luck,
Rain will fall on each of us,
But God is always just.

He gives us trials to make us strong,
He knows just what it takes,
But then when we rely on Him,
The storm begins to break.

Author: Betty H. Caldwell

Matthew 5:45 ". . . for he maketh his sun to rise on the evil and on the good, and sendeth rain on the just and on the unjust."

Trees

The trees are quickly undressing,
Getting ready for a long winter sleep,
Their pretty, little clothes are falling,
To cover their strong, steady feet.

Each one tells a story of beauty,
From spring unto winter, I've heard,
In spring, they give us their blossoms,
In winter, give shelter to birds.

They bow to the wind when it's stormy,
They tremble and chill when it's cold,
Sometimes, they grow weak and will stumble,
They are somewhat like us, I am told.

Like trees, we too are all different,
We each have a purpose in life,
So hold to His Hand when it's stormy,
He'll get you through winter and strife.

Author: Betty H. Caldwell

Leviticus 26:4 "Then I will give you rain in due season, and the land shall give her increase, and the trees of the field shall yield their fruit."

A Faithful Friend

It's always good to have a friend,
On whom you can depend,
A friend who's there through thick and thin,
And stays until the end.

You won't find many in this life,
Their number will be few,
They'll stay with you when all is well,
But vanish like the dew.

But, there's one friend who'll always stay,
Until the bitter end,
His name is Jesus Christ, my Lord,
There is no better friend.

His love for you is endless,
He gave His life for you,
He only wants your trust and love,
His love is tried and true.

Author: Betty H. Caldwell

John 15:13 "Greater love hath no man than this, that a man lay down his life for his friends."

Friends

Our friends are like a pretty bouquet,
Who enter our lives each day,
Some may be real and some may be silk,
Each beautiful in their way.

There's some I've known a lifetime,
Their memories are so dear,
And some are new and just as sweet,
With loyalty so dear.

God gave them for a reason,
Each one has touched my heart,
They're all a part of me, it seems,
Each day, somehow, a part.

So, each day treat them gently,
Each one's a special gem,
Be thankful for each one of them,
For they were sent by Him.

Author: Betty H. Caldwell

Proverbs 18:24 "A man that hath friends must shew himself friendly: and there is a friend that sticketh closer than a brother."

Master Potter

When as a little child at play,
The world was truly mine,
I had all that I needed,
I thought so, at that time.

Then one day I realized,
I needed more than me,
The needed help was Jesus,
I fell down on my knees.

He is a special friend of mine,
No other can compare,
He knows about my faults and then,
He listens to my prayers.

He knows me for He made me,
And I am just His clay,
He is the Master Potter,
I'll be with Him one day.

Author: Betty H. Caldwell

Isaiah 64:8 "But now, O Lord, thou art our father; we are the clay, and thou our potter; and we all are the work of thy hand."

My Friend

The sun peaks through as dawn arrives,
And showers have sprinkled the grass,
The bunnies, squirrels, and bluebirds,
Are waking and yawning at last.

My world is at peace this morning,
And comfort resides in my soul,
My Lord will always be with me,
I know for He said, it is so.

A true friend is there when he's needed,
Just call Him and He will be near,
If, by your friends, you're forsaken,
Just call on the One Satan fears.

He'll comfort and hold you forever,
He'll wipe all the tears from your face,
He'll stay by your side when you need Him,
And sadness and tears, He'll erase.

Author: Betty H. Caldwell

Proverbs 12:26 "The righteous is more excellent than his neighbor; but the way of the wicked seduceth them."

Always Remembered

You left us way too early,
Your life had just begun,
Though sadness fills my heart inside,
Your battle has been won.

I'll see your smile as clouds drift by,
As winds whisper your name,
I need not look too far away,
For part of you remains.

I'll feel your presence always,
And your laugh will always be,
The sound in every wave that breaks,
In pebbles by the sea.

Although I miss your smiling face,
And all the joy you gave,
I know that out there somewhere,
There's life beyond the grave.

Author: Betty H. Caldwell

John 14: 1 - 2 " Let not your heart be troubled: ye believe in God believe also in me. In my Father's house are many mansions: if it were not so, I would have told . . . "

A Memory

The loss of someone dear to us,
Leaves aching in our hearts,
No matter what our friends may say,
The pain will not depart.

They say that time will make a way,
To ease the wounded heart,
But time has passed so slowly,
Since we have been apart.

Your smiling face will always be,
A memory I will cling to,
Your voice, I'll hear inside the wind,
Your touch, in morning dew.

Our Father made a way for us,
To meet again one day,
The sacrifice was His own Son,
Whose blood has paved the way.

Author: Betty H. Caldwell

Psalm 30:5 "For his anger endureth but a moment, in his favor is life: weeping may endure for a night, but joy cometh in the morning."

Grace and Grief

Sooner or later we each will have,
A visitor called Grief,
He tends to knock on each one's door,
As surely as we speak.

But Grief won't be alone that day,
For Grace will be there too,
And it will make you stronger,
For Grace gives strength to you.

Our great Redeemer saw the need,
To save the sinful man,
He knew we could not save ourselves,
With Grace, He made a plan.

He looked at us with Mercy,
And said, I'll send My Son,
He'll take your sins upon His Cross,
With Grace, your battle's won.

Author: Betty H. Caldwell

2 Corinthians 12:9 "And he said unto me, My grace is sufficient for thee: for my strength is made perfect in weakness, . . . "

Home at Last

Each time I hear the Lord has called,
Another loved one home,
The hurt is deep within my soul,
My heart feels so alone.

One by one, they're called away,
To gain a heavenly home,
And I will miss each smiling face,
And pray God keeps me strong.

Their work on Earth is finished,
Their battles here are past,
They're safely in His arms of love,
And they're at home at last.

Although I'll miss them dearly,
I know they're happy there,
I wouldn't have them here again,
They're in the Father's care.

Author: Betty H. Caldwell

Matthew 25:46 "And these shall go away into everlasting punishment: but the righteous into life eternal."

Hope Will Return

When will my heart sing again?
When will my joy return?
Seems sadness has moved in to stay,
My grief is so deep and I yearn.

I can't bear this pain all alone,
Where is my comfort this time?
Just help me to weather this storm,
And show me a peace that is mine.

I know You are holding me close,
In Your arms for comfort, I'll stay,
Your strength is all that I have,
To face each new breaking day.

But someday, my life here will change,
I'll be with my Savior above,
There'll be no more sorrow or tears,
I'll be with the ones that I love.

Author: Betty H. Caldwell

John 16:20 ". . . that ye shall weep and lament, but the world shall rejoice: and ye shall be sorrowful, but your sorrow shall be turned into joy."

Life's Path

I started down a path one day,
When I was just a baby,
Back then no choice was mine to make,
No roads, no turns, no maybes.

I left my mother's knee for school,
Her tears were there to see,
She prayed that I'd be safe and sound,
And I'd return at three.

Then I grew up and left my home,
Green mountains far behind,
The seashore was my destiny,
But home was on my mind.

In passing years, loved ones have gone,
To meet Him and be blest,
But someday, we'll join holy hands,
And gain eternal rest.

Author: Betty H. Caldwell

Ecclesiastes 1:7 "All the rivers run into the sea; yet the sea is not full; unto the place from whence the rivers come, thither they return again."

Missing You

My heart is crying deep inside,
A part of it is gone,
Although the world's still turning,
And life must still go on.

Each time we suffer loss of those,
We've loved so very much,
A part of us dies with them,
We sadly miss their touch.

But memories stay with us,
They'll always be a part,
Although we cannot touch them,
They're always in our hearts.

But one day we will see them,
In a brighter side of life,
The sun and moon aren't needed,
For Jesus is the Light.

Author: Betty H. Caldwell

Matthew 5:4 "Blessed are they that mourn: for they shall be comforted."

My Dad

A lonely star was shining,
The night my dad went home,
He left us here that Christmas Day,
To go where he belonged.

He knew he would be leaving,
He was ready to meet The Son,
As he prayed upon his bedside,
He said, Your Will be done.

I know he's with the angels,
His sin was in the past,
The "Empty Mansion" that he sang,
Is finally his at last.

The spot he filled is empty,
He'll never be replaced,
But someday, I will see him,
And kiss his smiling face.

Author: Betty H. Caldwell

John 14:2 "In my Father's house are many mansions: if it were not so, I would have told you. I go to prepare a place for you."

Our Family Circle

Our circle now is broken,
Because you said goodbye,
I wanted so to keep you,
And now, I just ask why.

Through all the tears and heartache,
I know the Lord knew best,
He'll take us when the time is right,
And hold us to His breast.

Your face, your smile, I won't forget,
They'll always be a part,
Of me, in which you left behind,
Engraved upon my heart.

You left a void that can't be filled,
No one can take your place,
I'll miss you 'til He calls me home,
'Til then, He'll give me grace.

Author: Betty H. Caldwell

2 Samuel 12:23 "But now he is dead, wherefore should I fast? Can I bring him back again? I shall go to him, but he shall not return to me."

Take Time

Old memories are so precious,
Just like the old song goes,
Sometimes we do not take the time,
To stop and smell the rose.

Each year, another's missing,
We never had a clue,
We might not get the chance again,
To tell them, I love you.

So hold your loved ones close,
There may soon come a day,
When you can never say to them,
The words you want to say.

For life is like a vapor,
God tells us this is so,
So cherish every moment here,
And let your loved ones know.

Author: Betty H. Caldwell

James 4: 14 "Whereas ye know not what shall be on the morrow. For what is your life? It is even a vapour, that appeareth for a little time and then vanisheth away."

Trust Him

Sometimes, we just can't understand,
Why some things have to be,
Like giving up a loved one,
It's hard for us to see.

God said His thoughts and ways,
Are higher than our own,
Someday, we'll understand it all,
When we are at His throne.

He always has a reason,
Although we may not see,
He knows just when the time is right,
A lesson, it might be.

To each, He gives a purpose,
Sometimes, it's two or three,
But when your work on earth is done,
His Glory, you will see.

Author: Betty H. Caldwell

Isaiah 55:9 "For as the heavens are higher than the earth, so are my ways higher than your ways, and my thoughts than your thoughts."

We'll Meet Again

I wanted to stay forever,
The day God called me home,
I knew your tears would flow for me,
And you would feel alone.

But memories last forever,
And no one can deny,
They'll comfort you as your heart cries,
And keep me by your side.

But parting's not forever,
I'll see you once again,
I'll wait beside the Eastern Gate,
As Jesus lets you in.

So live for Him while you still can,
Don't waste it with your tears,
We'll meet again some distant day,
Rejoicing through the years.

Author: Betty H. Caldwell

Matthew 5:4 "Blessed are they that mourn: for they shall be comforted."

God's Flowers

Pretty flowers bloom in spring,
But only for the season,
Their beauty is a gift from God,
To us, without a reason.

In winter, they will rest,
But they shall soon return,
To bloom again the coming spring,
So please, don't ever yearn.

God made the pretty flowers,
To bring us joy and love,
They speak of His great love for us,
From Heaven up above.

So please, don't ever cry,
When they wither in the fall,
You'll see once again,
In just no time at all.

(Continued)

Our loved ones are the same,
God knows just what we need,
They're just like all the flowers,
He gives to us as seeds.

He lends them all to us,
To bless us in His way,
They prove to us, He lives,
And loves us every day.

Author: Betty H. Caldwell

Isaiah 40:8 "The grass withereth, the flower fadeth: but the word of our God will stand forever."

What Happened?

My heart is grieved today,
While listening to the news,
It speaks of evil so profound,
What happened to His rules?

Our hearts are getting numb, it seems,
Some think that sin is great,
Why, even some believers feel,
That God is out-of-date.

Where is the "Rock of Ages?"
Where is "Amazing Grace?"
I still love singing old-time hymns,
That brought me to this place.

My mom and dad both sang them,
And my grandparents too,
Some things can't be made better,
No matter what you do.

Author: Betty H. Caldwell

Romans 12:2 "And be not conformed to this world: but be ye transformed by the renewing of your mind, that ye may prove what is that good, and acceptable, and . . ."

His Crown

Our Savior wore a crown of thorns,
Upon His precious head,
They pressed against His brow and then,
He suffered as He bled.

His trial was just a circus,
In Him, no fault was found,
But Satan had to have his day,
So, Jesus Christ was bound.

They marched Him to Mount Calvary,
They would not set Him free,
They mocked Him there and spit on Him,
And nailed Him to the tree.

A crown of thorns He wore that day,
That never more will be,
When He comes back the second time,
He'll be our Glorious King.

Author: Betty H. Caldwell

Matthew 27:29 "And when they had plaited a crown of thorns, they put it upon his head, and a reed in his right hand: and they bowed the knee before him, and . . ."

Our Hope

Lord, I trust Your mercy,
Rejoice in Your salvation,
I pray that You will hear my prayer,
With mercy, heal our nation.

You said they would reject You,
And this we all have learned,
But Lord, there still are many,
Who wait for Your return.

I pray our nation's leaders,
Will turn to You again,
To lead us back to greatness,
The way You did back then.

It's then and only then,
We'll prosper and endure,
Dear Lord, if You will help us,
With You, we'll be secure.

Author: Betty H. Caldwell

2 Chronicles 7:14 "If my people, who are called by my name, shall humble themselves, and pray, and seek my face, and turn from their wicked ways, . . ."

My Strength

Oh Lord, my heart is heavy,
I know that You will see me through,
Please give me strength to bear this trouble,
My life, my hope, depends on you.

You're always there just when I need you,
I've called on You so many times,
Now, Lord, once more, just bring me comfort,
Please put Your healing hand in mine.

I'll trust You, Lord, in all my trials,
I know You'll never let me down,
I'll cling to You and never leave You,
I know that I am heaven-bound.

Please make my life down here a blessing,
And may I count each day for you,
I'll live for You with all my heart, Lord,
I know Your strength will take me through.

Author: Betty H. Caldwell

Psalm 46:1 "God is our refuge and strength, a very present help in trouble."

Temptation

When you're feeling tempted,
Old Satan says, give in,
Besides, no one will ever know,
Should you decide to sin.

No one will know what you have done,
So don't you fret at all,
It's just an itty, bitty sin,
Don't worry if you fall.

Small sins lead to big ones,
In just no time at all,
You'll find yourself in quicksand,
With Satan, when you fall.

If you will call upon the Lord,
His strength will make a way,
For you to flee from Satan,
There is no other way.

Author: Betty H. Caldwell

1 Corinthians 10:13 ". . . but God is faithful, who will not suffer you to be tempted above that ye are able, but will with the temptation also make a way to escape, . . ."

The Battle

The little birds stopped singing,
When Christ died on the cross,
Their little hearts were broken,
For such a tragic loss.

As darkness fell throughout the land,
The ground began to quiver,
The temple veil was rent in twain,
And all began to tremble.

Old Lucifer was happy,
For just a little while,
He thought he'd won the battle,
And thought he could defile.

But Satan's heart was broken,
As he came at last to see,
The tomb of Christ was empty,
He'd won the victory.

Author: Betty Caldwell

1 Corinthians 15:57 "But thanks be to God, which giveth us the victory through our Lord Jesus Christ."

The Only Hope

When my heart is breaking,
There's someone I can call,
He always wipes my tears away,
And holds me when I fall.

He understands my heartache,
He knows my every care,
He knows just why I'm hurting,
For me, He's always there.

You too can feel God's presence,
If only you believe,
He'll shadow you in arms of love,
His comfort, you'll receive.

So, never think all hope is gone,
Just give your life to Him,
Just open up your heart today,
And let him enter in.

Author: Betty H. Caldwell

Romans 8:24 "For we are saved by hope: but hope that is seen is not hope: for what a man seeth, why doth he yet hope for?"

A Christmas Gift

The world was dark before He came,
A tiny baby boy,
And few would recognize His name,
Or see Him as a joy.

A little boy, He became,
His family loved Him so,
He learned to be a carpenter,
His mother watched Him grow.

He taught us how to live and love,
A part of God's great plan,
He gave His life for you and me,
And saved the sinful man.

Although they crucified my Lord,
They never knew Him then,
He asked God to forgive them,
A love unknown to man.

Author: Betty H. Caldwell

Luke 1:35 ". . . and the power of the Highest shall overshadow thee: therefore also that holy thing which shall be born of thee shall be called the Son of God."

A Mother's Love

As Mary wept beneath the cross,
Her heart was in God's Hand,
She was the same as we would be,
She could not understand.

As Jesus looked on Mary's face,
His look showed how He loved her,
He said to her, behold your son,
To John, behold your mother.

A mother has unending love,
Her children, she loves so,
She'll give her life for each of them,
For each, she loves the "most."

So mothers, love your children,
Raise them to run His race,
Obey the Words He gave to you,
And they will seek His face.

Author: Betty H. Caldwell

John 19:26 "When Jesus therefore saw his mother, and the disciple standing by, whom he loved, he saith unto his mother, Woman, behold thy son."

Doubt

Doubting is an easy road,
And effort, it takes little,
Just think the worst of others,
And don't show any pity.

You'll find yourself alone one day,
And wonder what went wrong,
Why no one seems to care for you,
Your hurt will be so strong.

For no man is an island,
Alone upon the sea,
True fellowship is needed,
But some can never see.

But Christ will show you how to love,
And how a friend to be,
He'll show you how to love yourself,
Just trust in Him, you'll see.

Author: Betty H. Caldwell

1 Timothy 2:8 "I will therefore that men pray every where, lifting up holy hands, without wrath and doubting."

He Must Be First

He said to love your neighbor,
Just as you love yourself,
Before you can do just as He said,
Take God from off the shelf.

Then place Him in your heart,
And let Him always stay,
He'll fill your heart with so much love,
You must give some away.

You may think it's hard to do,
To put Him in first place,
But if He's put where He belongs,
He'll give you more than grace.

He'll give you peace of mind, no doubt,
He'll teach you how to live,
He'll free your soul from chains of sin,
Your new life will begin.

Author: Betty H. Caldwell

Matthew 6:33 "But seek ye first the kingdom of God, and his
righteousness: and all these things shall be added unto you."

Unchanging Love

Seasons come and seasons go,
They change throughout the year,
Winter, spring, summer, fall,
It's just God's plan, that's clear.

It's not for us to fret about,
For He knows everything,
He knows just what we need, and when,
Like when to send the rain.

The love of God will never change,
On that, we can rely,
He loves us each and every day,
We sometimes wonder why.

Our friends are like the seasons,
They may be there, or not,
But we can always count on God,
Who loves no matter what.

Author: Betty H. Caldwell

Malachi 3:6 "For I am the Lord, I change not; therefore ye sons of Jacob are not consumed."

Humility

Our Lord was very humble,
From the moment of His birth,
No other child I know of,
Was born this way on Earth.

Although He was a King,
He was a servant too,
He washed the feet of others,
His love came shining through.

He suffered on the cross,
With agony and strife,
He humbly bowed His head and died,
And fully paid our price.

Not one of us could do,
What Jesus did that day,
He only wants our love for Him,
And for us to obey.

Author: Betty H. Caldwell

Ephesians 4:2 "With all lowliness and meekness, with long suffering, forbearing one another in love."

Little Furry Ones

A kind heart not only loves others,
But loves little furry ones too,
For they all belong to the Master,
And they share His love just like you.

The old stray dog who looks hungry,
Or the kitten who just wants a home,
They can't find the words just to tell you,
They're so tired of being alone.

They have so much love just to give you,
And thankful to you, they will be,
For all that they want is to please you,
In you, their world, they will see.

If you're feeling sad this Christmas,
And tired of being alone,
Just share your heart with God's creatures,
He'll bless you with joy unknown.

Author: Betty H. Caldwell

Proverbs 12: 10 "A righteous man regardeth the life of his beast: but the tender mercies of the wicked are cruel."

My Mother

My mother's love is so profound,
She nurtures those she loves,
She's always there to meet our needs,
She's God's gift from above.

She sacrificed throughout her life,
And we were always fed,
Read stories each night by an old oil lamp,
When sick, she sat by our bed.

She wiped our tears when we would cry,
And defended us from harm,
Humility belonged to her,
With beauty, love and charm.

She is the anchor of her home,
Her faith is so abundant,
A crown she'll wear in Glory,
For in this life, she earned it.

Author: Betty H. Caldwell

Isaiah 49: 15 "Can a woman forget her suckling child, that she should not have compassion on the son of her womb? yea, they may forget, yet will I not forget thee."

No Greater Love

Lord, my home is humble,
A castle, it is not,
It's just a place to lay my head,
A warm and welcome spot.

An earthly home, our Lord had none,
No place to lay His head,
But He had many mansions,
He chose to leave instead.

No greater love could ever be,
Than that He had for me,
For me, He died upon the cross,
That rugged, lonely tree.

My heart breaks just in knowing,
The price He paid that day,
Just when it seemed all hope was gone,
The stone was rolled away.

Author: Betty H. Caldwell

Matthew 8:20 "And Jesus saith unto him, the foxes have holes, and the birds of the air have nests; but the Son of man hath not where to lay his head."

Ode to Hanna

Hanna is a beagle,
With long and floppy ears,
A nose that misses nothing,
And an appetite to fear.

A heart as big as Heaven,
And love that never ends,
She's more than just a dog to me,
She is my little friend.

She fills a special spot, it seems,
A need within my heart,
I love her in so many ways,
To count, I could not start.

I know God sent her to me,
To ease my tears, like rain,
When Little Chief and Wendi left,
God knew she'd ease the pain.

Author: Betty H. Caldwell

Psalm 50: 10-11 "For every beast of the forest is mine, and the cattle upon a thousand hills. I know all the fowls of the mountains, and the wild beasts of the field . . ."

Remembering Christmas

I remember Christmas Day,
When just a little girl,
I always wanted fancy things,
Like dolls and bikes and pearls.

My family then could not afford,
To buy those fancy joys,
I watched as others came to play,
And show off all their toys.

I couldn't understand it then,
Why Santa never came,
I thought I had been good enough,
For him to have my name.

But we had something more than toys,
This world could never know,
Our home had love and laughter,
That only God bestows.

Author: Betty H. Caldwell

Zephaniah 3:17 "The Lord thy God in the midst of thee is mighty: he will save, he will rejoice over thee with joy: he will rest in his love, he will joy over thee with singing."

Summer

The butterflies are sipping,
Their nectar from each rose,
The mockingbirds are winging,
And singing summer's prose.

The dragonflies are darting,
As summer fills the air,
The honeybees are golden,
With pollen from each flower.

Oh, what a glorious day it is,
Enjoy it while it lasts,
For wintertime is coming,
And summer will be past.

I thank You Lord for summer,
And wintertime as well,
For us, you made the seasons,
Your love for us they tell.

Author: Betty H. Caldwell

Genesis 8:22 "While the earth remaineth, seedtime and harvest, and cold and heat, and summer and winter, and day and night shall not cease."

The Dove

The dove is very special,
It's innocent and sweet,
Its song can change the morning,
From quiet to sweet replete.

Each creature has a purpose,
On earth, and each a season,
God thought of everything to be,
He always has a reason.

God uses them to do His Will,
Dominion, He gave man,
He loves all His creation,
It's all in His great plan.

Noah sent a dove one day,
To find dry ground for feeding,
He knew that if the dove returned,
There'd be no food for eating.

(Continued)

He waited still and sent again,
The dove to look about,
Then she returned and in her beak,
An olive leaf, no doubt.

Author: Betty Caldwell

Genesis 8:8 "Also he sent forth a dove from him, to see if the waters were abated from off the face of the ground."

The Gardener

A loyal gardener loves his plants,
And cares for them each day,
He gently waters, tills, and feeds,
And takes the weeds away.

Just as the gardener loves the rose,
The Lord so loves us too,
He often gives us sunshine,
Sometimes, a storm or two.

So, if you pray and don't receive,
It may not be His will,
He sometimes grants our wishes,
Your needs, He'll always fill.

So always trust Him when you pray,
He's sure to answer still,
It may be soon, or later,
Your needs, He'll always fill.

Author: Betty H. Caldwell

Philippians 4: 19 "But my God shall supply all your need according to his riches in glory by Christ Jesus."

The Gift

Our Lord has given many gifts,
Of this, we all can see,
But the greatest gift He gave of all,
Was His Son at Calvary.

They crucified my Lord that day,
Oh, what a tragedy,
The innocent Lamb of God who died,
Who gave His life for me.

Someday, I want to tell Him,
How much He means to me,
When face-to-face I meet Him,
And worship at His feet.

Lord, while I walk this troubled earth,
Just help me find the way,
To point someone to follow You,
And live for You each day.

Author: Betty H. Caldwell

John 3: 16 "For God so loved the world that he gave his only begotten son, that whosoever believeth in him, should not perish but have everlasting life."

The Lily of the Valley

A pretty flower bloomed one day,
Called Lily of the Valley,
It spoke to all who came its way,
It was the spring finale.

Again, next spring, it rose again,
To prove it could be done,
It spread its seed throughout the land,
And multiplied from one.

Our Savior came upon the Earth,
To tell us how that we,
Could be with Him some distant day,
Beside the crystal sea.

He is the Lily of the Valley,
He rose just like the flower,
He's coming back again someday,
In all His might and power.

Author: Betty H. Caldwell

Song of Solomon 2: 1 "I am the rose of Sharon, and the lily of the valleys."

The Road to Home

It's said, You can't go home again,
That nothing is the same,
It's true that all is different,
But love will never change.

Our homes may change in many ways,
And loved ones change some too,
But love grows deeper through the years,
A lot depends on you.

Our home on Earth is temporal,
It may not last too long,
But our home above is eternal,
With God, you can't go wrong.

Be patient 'til the Master,
Decides to bring you home,
It may be soon, or later,
So, you keep holding on.

Author: Betty H. Caldwell

John 14:2 "In my Father's house are many mansions: if it were not so, I would have told you. I go to prepare a place for you."

Autumn

Autumn is a glorious time,
As leaves begin to change,
To yellow, gold, and purple,
And shout God's Holy Name.

The breeze tells them it's time to fall,
And rest again 'til spring,
And let the flowers go to sleep,
And have sweet dreams of rain.

Sometimes the summer lingers,
And just won't go away,
But God who made the seasons,
Will always have His way.

In fall, we rest our weary heads,
And live in sweet respite,
Enjoy its beauty while it lasts,
And in its peace, delight.

Author: Betty H. Caldwell

Ecclesiastes 3: 1 "To everything there is a season, and a time to every purpose under the heaven;"

Don't Worry

When you wake up this morning,
And raise your sleepy head,
Just look outside your window,
There's something to be said.

The sun is brightly shining,
The sky is pristine blue,
A little cloud is drifting by,
And God's still loving you.

Don't stop and dwell on yesterday,
Just let your sorrows end,
Don't worry about tomorrow,
For God says it is His.

Just lift your hands and praise Him,
He deserves your very best,
Just give to Him your future,
Relax, and worry less.

Author: Betty H. Caldwell

Matthew 6:34 "Take therefore no thought for the morrow: for the morrow shall take thought for the things of itself. Sufficient unto the day is the evil thereof."

My Comforter

Some days a cloud will hide the sun,
While tears flow just like rain,
When those we love have let us down,
And life's just not the same.

Sometimes, the ones we love the most,
Can break our hearts in two,
It seems no matter what we do,
The pain is through and through.

But there is one who wipes the tears,
And mends the broken-hearted,
He'll stay with you through shattered dreams,
Until your pain has parted.

He'll comfort you when loss is great,
And hold your hand forever,
His name is Jesus Christ, The Lord,
And He will leave you never.

Author: Betty H. Caldwell

John 14:16 "And I will pray the Father, and he shall give you another Comforter, that he may abide with you for ever;"

My King

The breeze became a whisper,
As rain came softly down,
The sky was dark as indigo,
The stars could not be found.

I felt a loneliness inside,
A void I could not fill,
I'd searched for earthly treasures,
But that was not His Will.

For God has known me always,
But I'd rejected Him,
I thought about my life of sin,
My eyes with tears grew dim.

I felt my broken spirit,
Fill up with grief and pain,
I knew I'd found my treasure,
At last, I'd met my King.

Author: Betty H. Caldwell

Deuteronomy 4:29 "But if from thence thou shalt seek the Lord thy God, thou shalt find him, if thou seek him with all thy heart and with all thy soul."

Our Keeper

The joy I feel inside my heart,
The comfort in my soul,
Just knowing that I am His child,
Brings peace to me untold.

I know not what tomorrow brings,
So, I'll just do my best,
To honor Jesus Christ, my King,
And leave to Him the rest.

He knows each time a sparrow falls,
And knows my every need,
He'll lead me daily as I live,
While on His Word, I feed.

So put your trust in Jesus,
On Him, you can depend,
He'll place a hedge around you,
And keep you 'til the end.

Author: Betty H. Caldwell

2 Thessalonians 3:3 "But the Lord is faithful, who shall stablish
you and keep you from evil."

Peace

The birds are singing in the trees,
The sky is still so blue,
We pray for peace throughout the world,
But it's not coming true.

If we would only listen,
To what God says to do,
There would be peace upon the Earth,
The Bible still is true.

We must tell others about Christ,
And what He did for us,
He'll give us peace within our hearts,
If only we will trust.

So let's join hearts together,
And pray that souls are saved,
And wait until our Lord returns,
To take His Bride away.

Author: Betty H. Caldwell

John 16:33 "These things I have spoken unto you, that in me ye might have peace. In the world ye shall have tribulation: but be of good cheer; I have overcome the world."

Silence

Did you ever watch a falling star,
How silently it falls,
It quickly streaks across the sky,
We hear no sound at all.

Or watch the moon as it comes up,
And moves across the sky,
Our Lord knew we would need it,
To give a brilliant light.

Be still and know that I am God,
He knew we needed peace,
He had to tell us to be quiet,
So we could hear Him speak.

We need to have some quiet time,
To talk to God each day,
But mostly, we should listen,
To what God has to say.

Author: Betty H. Caldwell

Psalm 46: 10 "Be still, and know that I am God: I will be exalted among the heathen, I will be exalted in the earth."

Sweet Autumn

The grass sways softly in the wind,
The fields of grain unnumbered,
The flowers whisper their goodbyes,
As summer starts to slumber.

There's certain peace this time of year,
When all take time to rest,
The leaves are slowly drifting down,
They seem to feel it best.

But some things keep on going,
The moon still sheds its light,
The rivers are still rushing by,
The mountains are a sight.

And God is still in heaven,
He sits upon His throne,
All things are as they should be,
As autumn sings its song.

Author: Betty H. Caldwell

Ecclesiastes 3: 11 "He hath made every thing beautiful in his time: also he hath set the world in their heart, so that no man can find out the work that God maketh . . ."

Father of Creation

Let us sing unto the Lord,
Lift our voices in our joy,
Let us sing in sweet refrain,
For we know that Jesus reigns.

Let the mountains shout His Name,
While the rivers do the same,
Let the pretty bluebells ring,
For He is their Glorious King.

Let the oceans and the seas,
Birds and fish and bumble bees,
Shout their praises and their glee,
Christ is still their Holy King.

Let the lilies and the trees,
Bow their heads beneath the breeze,
While they sing a song of praise,
Let their holy anthems raise.

Author: Betty H. Caldwell

Psalm 66:4 "All the earth shall worship thee, and shall sing unto thee; they shall sing to thy name. Selah"

His Feet

He walked the dusty road one day,
To Calvary, He trod,
His feet were dusty, tired, and sore,
His blood fell on the sod.

Though we say much about His Hands,
And true, they are amazing,
He formed the world from nothing,
Made heavens for our gazing.

He never traveled far from home,
But still, He reached us all,
His footprints touched so many hearts,
And many heard His call.

His Feet will touch this world again,
In power, not defeat,
They'll shine like brass, and all shall see,
We'll worship at His Feet.

Author: Betty H. Caldwell

John 12:3 "Then took Mary a pound of ointment of spikenard, very costly, and anointed the feet of Jesus, and wiped his feet with her hair; and the house was filled . . ."

97

His Hands

His Hands created the heavens,
His Hands created the seas,
With care, He created the mountains,
With love, He created me.

His Hands healed the sick in the Bible,
His Hands made the lame walk again,
There's nothing His Hands cannot master,
He saved mortal man from his sin.

How can you not see Him as I see,
He's the Lord over all in this Earth,
He's owned it all since creation,
He's owned all of us since our birth.

So honor Him as Creator,
All heaven and earth lift His Name,
So praise Him just like the angels,
And worship the King, for He reigns.

Author: Betty H. Caldwell

Job 12:10 "In whose hand is the soul of every living thing, and the breath of all mankind."

His Splendor

His splendor covers the heavens,
Much more than we'll ever see,
He owns the cattle of a thousand hills,
And also owns you and me.

He owns the Earth and all it has,
Our treasures, too, are His,
You did not do it all alone,
He owns it all while you live.

Without Him, we'd be nothing,
For we'd be lost in our sin,
He gave His life just to save us,
If we'll just let Him in.

So, give Him praise each day you live,
We owe Him so much more,
We owe Him everything we have,
He's knocking at your door.

Author: Betty H. Caldwell

Deuteronomy 10:14 "Behold the heaven and the heaven of heavens is the Lord's thy God, the earth also, with all that therein is."

Mighty Father

The stars are in the heavens,
The sun is in its place,
Creation's still in order,
But not the human race.

The tide still ebbs and flows,
The mountain peaks are tall,
The leaves are turning gold again,
I look at them in awe.

The sky is blue this morning,
The pines are growing tall,
It seems that all is well with us,
But that's not so, at all.

For mankind has forgotten,
Who made the mountain peaks,
Some say that they have just evolved,
That God just didn't speak.

Author: Betty H. Caldwell

Psalm 33:9 "For he spake and it was done; he commanded and it stood fast."

My Everything

The grass will always wither,
And the flowers always fade,
God's Word will stand forever,
So, do not be dismayed.

He knew you from before,
There was an Earth and sun,
He loved you as a sinner,
Now loves you as His son.

So, always trust in Jesus,
He'll never let you down,
He'll give you peace and comfort,
His love will still abound.

A friend when you are lonely,
A Comforter with peace,
A healer when you need Him,
A Savior, wants to be.

Author: Betty H. Caldwell

Jeremiah 1:5 "Before I formed thee in the belly I knew thee; and before thou camest forth out of the womb, I sanctified thee, and I ordained thee a prophet . . ."

My God is Awesome

The smiling face of a baby,
A fawn running through the glade,
The miracle of a bumble bee,
It's an awesome world You made.

The moon and stars so high above,
The mountains and the seas,
I'm overcome with wonder,
And think, how can this be?

You spoke, and all existed,
Though some do not believe,
The Holy Bible says it's so,
And that's enough for me.

You healed the blind and raised the dead,
Why can't this world just see,
That You're the only One True God,
With miracles for me.

Author: Betty H. Caldwell

Psalm 40:5 "Many, O Lord my God, are thy wonderful works which thou has done, . . ."

Praise Him

The daisy raised its pretty face,
And thanked Him for its little space,
It thanked Him for the sun and rain,
And then it thanked Him for His grace.

I praise His Name for all to hear,
How much my Savior means to me,
I praise Him for my debt He paid,
The day they nailed Him on the tree.

Should I worry and anxious be,
Never, never, no, not me,
I have someone who cares for me,
He holds my hand and calms the sea.

So, little flowers trust in Him,
For He supplies your every need,
The same He does for us each day,
As daily, on His Word we feed.

Author: Betty H. Caldwell

Psalm 150:4 "Praise him with the timbrel and dance: praise him with stringed instruments and organs."

The Great I Am

Who commands the morning,
Who turns the tide each day,
And laid foundations of the Earth,
And taught us how to pray.

Who made the cloud a garment,
To swaddle us inside,
Who made the sun to warm us,
And give a light besides.

The morning stars all sing His Praise,
And shout His victory,
He gave us counsel in His Word,
If we would only heed.

Now Lord, I give my life to Thee,
To use it as You may,
You are the only One True God,
Forever and a day.

Author: Betty H. Caldwell

Isaiah 48: 13 "My hand also hath laid the foundation of the earth, and my right hand hath spanned the heavens: when I call unto them, they stand up together."

The Wonder of Him

I often wondered as a child,
What made the sky so blue,
And then one day I met the Lord,
Who taught me what was true.

He said He made the heavens,
And all the stars and moon,
He even made the grass so green,
And all the planets too.

He made the birds and cottontails,
The squirrels and raccoons too,
He made the ants and butterflies,
And seas and oceans blue.

I thought how awesome it must be,
To make the stars and sea,
But then I thought how awesome still,
That He made little me.

Author: Betty H. Caldwell

Genesis 2:7 "And the Lord God formed man of the dust of the ground, and breathed into his nostrils the breath of life; and man became a living soul."

Worship

God gave us a voice to sing praises,
He gave us our hands to pray,
He gave us our knees to bow down on,
Our feet are to follow each day.

For Jesus gave praise to the Father,
His hands often folded to pray,
He bowed on His knees and was holy,
His footsteps have shown us The Way.

Oh, Lord, I want to be worthy,
Let my life be used as You choose,
Just mold and make me Your vessel,
Your will, I cannot refuse.

Someday, when I'm living in heaven,
Your glorious face I will see,
The sun and the moon won't be needed,
For Your Light is all I will need.

Author: Betty H. Caldwell

1 John 1:7 "But if we walk in the light, as he is in the light, we have fellowship one with another, and the blood of Jesus Christ his Son cleanseth us from all sin."

Your Glory

The Earth is full of Your Glory,
From the mountaintops down to the sea,
It speaks of your great mighty power,
It shines for all here to see.

Man had his tower of Babel,
And all wonders here in this world,
But his wonders will never compare with,
A single, tiny white pearl.

You've given to me fresh, cool water,
And You've given me good food to eat,
You even gave to me Jesus,
To save my poor soul from defeat.

Your Hands are seen in creation,
Your work is everywhere I see,
I thank You for giving me wisdom,
When you gave the Bible to me.

Author: Betty H. Caldwell

2 Corinthians 3: 10 "For even that which was made glorious had no glory in this respect, by reason of the glory that excelleth."

Choices

The choices that we make,
Are sometimes very bad,
And when we see what happens,
We then feel very sad.

We think we know what's best for us,
Or that it doesn't matter,
If we would seek God's guidance first,
Our lives would be much better.

He wants us to depend on Him,
In all the things we do,
For big and little things, as well,
He knows what's best for you.

So, always ask Him for His help,
On what you do and say,
He'll always guard the steps you take,
And guide you all the way.

Author: Betty H. Caldwell

Psalm 25:4 "Show me thy ways, Oh Lord, teach me thy paths."

Dear God

Good morning, Loving Father,
Just want to talk with You,
It seems that when I call Your Name,
I'm always feeling blue.

Today, I don't want anything,
Just want to say, I love You,
And just to thank You for Your love,
That ever is so true.

You sent Your Son to die for me,
What more could You have done,
He paid a debt He didn't owe,
He was the only One.

So, Lord, I'll always bless Your Name,
There is no God but You,
I'll live my life for You each day,
And Grace will see me through.

Author: Betty H. Caldwell

Ephesians 5:20 "Giving thanks always for all things unto God and
the Father in the name of our Lord Jesus Christ."

For Bonnie

Lord, I ask You to be with me,
As I struggle day by day,
It seems each day gets harder,
And pain won't go away.

Old Satan tries to tell me,
That I may not survive,
But then, I pray and feel Your love,
And know that I'll be fine.

I know You'll be beside me,
No matter what will be,
Your strength will be my refuge,
Your promise is for me.

We'll get through this together,
My family, You, and I,
I'll hold onto Your loving Hand,
By grace, I will abide.

Author: Betty H. Caldwell

John 11:4 "When Jesus heard that, he said, This sickness is not unto death, but for the glory of God, that the Son of God might be glorified thereby."

He Listens

I cry out to the Lord,
His mercy is my prayer,
When burdens seem to overcome,
My Lord is always there.

He'll stay with us in sickness,
He'll stand by us in health,
His mercy and His love sustains,
In poverty and wealth.

He always listens closely,
When you approach His throne,
To Him, you're so important,
Don't think all hope is gone.

Just boldly tell Him of your need,
And pray if it's His Will,
He'll hear your prayer, for you're His child,
His love for you is real.

Author: Betty H. Caldwell

Psalm 142:1 "I cried unto the Lord with my voice; with my voice unto the Lord did I make my supplication."

His Will

A tender heart that's full of love,
Is fragile as can be,
Just like a piece of crystal,
It breaks so easily.

A little child with tears of pain,
Can melt the strongest heart,
While mothers try to ease the hurt,
Our Lord must play a part.

There's some things we can't understand,
It's just not meant to be,
But someday all will be revealed,
When Christ, our Lord, we see.

Just take your heartaches to His throne,
Just ask and you'll receive,
If it's His Will, and not your own,
But first, you must Believe.

Author: Betty H. Caldwell

1 Thessalonians 5: 18 "In every thing give thanks: for this is the will of God in Christ Jesus concerning you."

In His Presence

I lift my heart to you this day,
I know You're in control,
No matter what the world may say,
You own my very soul.

I pray that I can bless someone,
Somehow, throughout this day,
And that You'll guide my footsteps,
And keep me in Your way.

The snares prepared by Satan,
Will vanish in Your sight,
His time on Earth will soon be gone,
He'll vanish as the night.

So, Father, keep me close to You,
Don't ever let me stray,
Your love for me's eternal,
There is no other way.

Author: Betty H. Caldwell

James 4:8 "Draw nigh to God, and he will draw nigh to you. Cleanse your hands, ye sinners; and purify your hearts, ye double minded."

Morning Devotion

In the wee hours of the morning,
As dawn replaces night,
Just me and God together,
To start the day off right.

I tell Him that I'm thankful,
For all He's done, you see,
I tell Him that I love Him,
He gave His Son for me.

Then others, I remember,
That they will surely find,
The love that He can give them,
And blessed peace of mind.

I pray that You will keep us,
Safe in Your Arms of Love,
No matter what the world may say,
You are the God above.

Author: Betty H. Caldwell

Psalm 88: 13 "But unto thee have I cried, O Lord' and in the morning shall my prayer prevent thee."

Morning Prayer

As I awake this morning,
Please hold me in Your Hand,
Just keep me safe from danger,
And help me understand.

Your will is all I want to do,
I know it's Your great plan,
Just let my eyes be open,
To see what You command.

Your strength and love sustain me,
They're all I'll ever need,
But sometimes, Lord, I fail You,
Sometimes, I just can't see.

If I should slip and stumble,
I pray that You'll forgive,
Lord, help me to remember,
For You, I want to live.

Author: Betty H. Caldwell

1 John 1:9 "If we confess our sins, he is faithful and just to forgive us our sins, and to cleanse us from all unrighteousness."

Prayer

Lord, as I start each day anew,
I pray each one begins with You,
Please let my heart believe Your Word,
And let my soul know that You care.

Just like the sun and morning dew,
I know it all began with You,
You made the sun, I know that's true,
Creation proves to me, You're You.

So as I spend my day with You,
I pray my life shows honor too,
You gave Your all for me one day,
The least that I can do is pray.

And then each night when all is still,
I pray that I have done Your will,
And if I falter, please forgive,
Dear Lord, for You, I'll always live.

Author: Betty H. Caldwell

1 Thessalonians 5: 17-18 ". . . Pray without ceasing. In every thing give thanks; for this is the will of God in Christ Jesus concerning you."

Take Me Back

Lord, take me back to the good old days,
When the church belonged to You,
They sang and prayed and read Your Word,
And joy filled each pew.

The fear of God was given,
As the old time preacher prayed,
He made us want to live for You,
And share your love each day.

Today the church is social,
No talk of sin or hell,
And often neighbors will complain,
When someone rings the bells.

I guess that is progression,
And some might say, it's great,
But I just want my Savior,
As the center of my faith.

Author: Betty H. Caldwell

Romans 12:2 "And be not conformed to this world; but be ye transformed
by the renewing of your mind, . . . "

117

Fear

Our lives today are filled with fear,
And our dismay abounds,
No matter where we work or play,
It seems that fear is found.

Our children don't feel safe at school,
Our churches lock their gates,
What's happened in our land today,
To bring us to this state?

We never used to lock our doors,
Our children safely played,
We looked out for each other,
And in our homes, we prayed.

But God's no longer welcome,
We told Him, "Go away,
We'll call You if we need You,
We want things done our way."

Author: Betty H. Caldwell

2 Timothy 1:7 "For God hath not given us the spirit of fear; but of power, and of love, and of a sound mind."

Whole Armor of God

Each morning as the day breaks,
Old Satan wakes up too,
Deceit is foremost on his mind,
As he tries to get to you.

So put on God's whole armor,
Don't be caught by surprise,
Ask God to always keep you,
With strength as you abide.

Old Satan's always plotting,
To get you in some way,
Going to and fro throughout the Earth,
To destroy you someday.

But our God is omnipotent,
In Him, Our strength is found,
He'll always give protection,
And Satan will be bound.

Author: Betty H. Caldwell

Ephesians 6: 11 "Put on the whole armor of God, that ye may be able to stand against the wiles of the devil."

119

God, My Protector

Today, I rose up from my rest,
With peace and joy within,
Then heard the news and felt depressed,
The world's so full of sin.

Satan strives with all his might,
To drive us far away,
From Christ who paid it all for us,
Don't let him have his way.

Our Lord is always in control,
He'll guard you day and night,
He'll put a hedge around you,
And keep you in His sight.

So, when you're weary of this world,
Don't think you are alone,
For God is always with you,
His love will keep you strong.

Author: Betty H. Caldwell

Psalm 91:4 "He shall cover thee with his feathers, and under his wings shall thou trust: his truth shall be thy shield and buckler."

He Goes Before Me

My enemies surround me,
Where do I go from here?
I know that God is with me,
And I should never fear.

Because I am a child of His,
With me, He'll always stay,
Now Lord, I really need you,
To take my hurt away.

When God's wrath falls on sinful man,
The mountains shake and tremble,
His voice will sound like thunder,
His judgment won't be gentle.

Don't ever hurt a child of His,
You'll never win the battle,
He'll always be there for His own,
Your reasons will not matter.

Author: Betty H. Caldwell

Matthew 28:20 "Teaching them to observe all things whatsoever I have commanded you: and, lo, I am with you alway, even unto the end of the world."

Peaceful Sleep

An evening breeze blows softly,
The sun is sinking low,
I see a star just peeking,
At all of us below.

The moon has said "hello" again,
The stars are shining brightly,
It seems that all is peace on Earth,
As we enjoy them nightly.

The birds have said goodnight to all,
And night is drawing near,
It'll soon be time to say "sweet dreams,"
So rest and feel secure.

God knew that we would need some time,
To rest our weary souls,
So dream in peaceful sleep tonight,
Your life's in His control.

Author: Betty H. Caldwell

Psalm 4:8 "I will both lay me down in peace, and sleep; for thou, Lord, only makest me dwell in safety."

He Never Slumbers

We guard our homes down here below,
Protecting things we love,
From thieves who plot to steal away,
Not trusting God above.

Our Lord is watching night and day,
To keep us safe from harm,
He never sleeps or slumbers,
So don't you be alarmed.

Your life is under His control,
He never goes away,
He watches as you fall asleep,
And knows when you awake.

So, as you rest your head tonight,
Just know He never sleeps,
He guards your soul and every breath,
Your life is His to keep.

Author: Betty H. Caldwell

Psalm 121:4 "Behold, he that keepeth Israel shall neither slumber nor sleep."

America, Turn Back

What happened to our country?
Where is our peace within?
We're in a downward spiral,
Where did it all begin?

Where is the family unit,
The children, moms, and dads?
Where is the grace we used to say,
Before we broke our bread.

Let's get back to the basics,
The way it used to be,
When families prayed together,
For all the world to see.

If we'd humble ourselves and pray,
Turn from our wicked ways,
Then He'd forgive our sins,
And heal our land today.

Author: Betty H. Caldwell

2 Chronicles 7:14 "If my people . . . and turn from their wicked ways;
then will I hear from heaven, and will forgive their sin, and will heal their
land."

All Your Heart

A man walked in a garden,
So weary and forlorn,
He thought about his life, so sad,
And why he had been born.

He said, I've been a cheater,
And maybe told some lies,
But never meant to hurt a soul,
Now Lord, I want to die.

I lost my loved ones and my friends,
I've led a life of sin,
Too late, I know I've made my fate,
Lord, you know where I've been.

He gave his heart to God that day,
Not just a part, but all,
The Lord gave him forgiveness,
Which He can do for all.

Author: Betty H. Caldwell

Luke 10:27 "... Thou shalt love the Lord thy God with all thy soul and with all thy heart ..."

A Sinner's Prayer

Lord, I am a sinner,
You know where I have been,
I pray that You'll forgive me,
And save my soul from sin.

I'll turn away from my old life,
New creature, I'll become,
I know You died and rose again,
So, I could be Your son.

I'll follow You in water,
You showed me how it's done,
My burdens will be lifted,
My hero is the Son.

Now, Father take and use me,
And help me day-by-day,
Please shelter me and keep me,
Forever in Your Way.

Author: Betty H. Caldwell

Romans 5:8 "But God commendeth his love toward us in that, while we were yet sinners, Christ died for us."

Don't You Forget

Don't you forget what God has done,
To bless you in this life,
And don't forget He died for you,
And suffered pain and strife.

Some say that God is dead today,
Or that He isn't real,
They live and do just what they please,
And say, it's no big deal.

Don't you forget He punished those,
Back in the ancient days,
Who disobeyed His Holy Word,
And challenged Godly ways.

He has not changed since long ago,
His judgment's still the same,
If you repent and change your ways,
He'll save you in His Name.

Author: Betty H. Caldwell

Isaiah 13:11 "And I will punish the world for their evil, and the wicked for their iniquity: and I will cause the arrogancy of the proud to cease, . . ."

Do You Know Him

I do not know that Jesus,
Peter said unto the maid,
And denied Him two times more,
Before the breaking day.

Now Peter loved the Lord,
But he was so afraid,
He didn't have the courage,
So Christ, he did betray.

He then recalled that Jesus said,
You will deny Me thrice,
Then Peter wept so bitterly,
But changed his heart that night.

Do you really know my Savior,
Or do you just pretend?
If you don't know Him in your heart,
Repent and let Him in.

Author: Betty H. Caldwell

John 18:17 "Then saith the damsel that kept the door unto Peter, Art thou not thou also one of this man's disciples? He saith, I am not."

Gethsemane

In the Garden of Gethsemane,
Alone, our Savior prayed,
He wanted them to watch and wait,
Asleep, instead they laid.

In fervent prayer, He prayed,
The Father's Will, not His,
He knew what He must suffer,
To save mankind from sin.

As drops of sweat fell from His Brow,
His blood was mingled in,
What agony He must have felt,
To triumph over sin.

How could you still not love Him,
The One who died for you?
He gave His all upon that cross,
To give you life that's new.

Author: Betty H. Caldwell

Mark 14:32 "And they came to a place which was named Gethsemane: and he saith to his disciples, sit ye here while I shall pray."

God Never Changes

It seems so much is changing,
In this old world below,
My head is spinning from the speed,
At which it seems to go.

Today, some say that right is wrong,
And wrong, these days, is right,
But that's not what the Bible says,
It's still the same, in spite.

God told us back in ancient days,
Just what to do and how,
His Word's the same, He hasn't changed,
His mind from then to now.

For sin is sin, no matter what,
The world is telling you,
Just give your life to Christ today,
His Word's forever true.

Author: Betty H. Caldwell

Hebrews 13:8 "Jesus Christ the same yesterday, and today, and forever."

Have You Met Him

Before you know the Father,
You must first know His Son,
So if you haven't met them,
I'll tell you how it's done.

Just have a talk with Jesus,
Repent, and tell Him so,
And turn your back on worldly sin,
Obedience to Him show.

Acknowledge that He died for you,
And rose from death again,
Just trust Him as your Savior,
Eternal life, you'll win.

Your blessings will be many,
And you'll gain peace of mind,
So, give your heart to Him today,
Eternal life, you'll find.

Author: Betty H. Caldwell

John 14:6 "Jesus saith unto him, I am the way, the truth, and the life: no man cometh unto the Father but by me."

Heavenly Thoughts

My thoughts cannot imagine,
What Heaven must be like,
With its magnitude of splendor,
And streets of pure delight.

The singing of the angels,
Their songs of sweet refrain,
The glorious throne my Lord adorns,
How glorious is His Name!

But most of all, I want to see,
The One who died for me,
I'll bow down low and worship,
And kiss His Holy Feet.

He wants to be your Savior too,
Your life is in His Hands,
Invite Him in just as you are,
Don't stand on sinking sands.

Author: Betty H. Caldwell

Revelation 21:18 "And the building of the wall of it was of jasper; and the city was pure gold, like unto clear glass."

Loneliness

When you're feeling lonely,
And weary from your load,
A friend is always waiting,
To share your lonely road.

He'll share your trials and troubles,
And listen as you cry,
He'll take your hand and lead you,
And stay close by your side.

He only wants your fellowship,
Your faithfulness and love,
He'll gladly wipe your tears away,
He'll bless you from above.

Just come to Him sincerely,
Repent and call His Name,
He'll wash your sins as white as snow,
You'll never be the same.

Author: Betty H. Caldwell

Deuteronomy 31:6 "Be strong and of a good courage, fear not, nor be afraid of them: for the Lord thy God, he it is that doth go with thee; . . ."

Living Water

As raindrops fall upon the grass,
The grass begins to grow,
The flowers stretch their heads and yawn,
Our Lord has made it so.

Rain is good for all things green,
God knew what He was planning,
He gave us every herb and seed,
The sun and soil for planting.

He later sent us Living Water,
His name is Jesus Christ,
He said we'd never thirst again,
Because He paid the price.

If you receive Him at His Word,
Fall on your knees and pray,
And take Him at His promise,
With you, He'll always stay.

Author: Betty H. Caldwell

John 4:14 "But whosoever drinketh of the water that I shall give him shall never thirst; but the water that I shall give him shall be in him a well of water . . ."

Mary

Mary, Mary, don't you cry,
You'll see your Son someday,
You'll see Him on His Great White Throne,
He'll wipe your tears away.

He was a young man when He left,
Just thirty years and three,
His work on Earth was finished,
As they nailed Him on the tree.

But He left those to carry on,
And finish His great plan,
He taught them what they had to do,
To save the sinful man.

He will return as our Great King,
Salvation's Plan complete,
All knees will bow before Him,
And worship at His Feet.

Author: Betty H. Caldwell

John 19:25 "Now there stood by the cross of Jesus his mother, and his mother's sister, Mary the wife of Cleophas, and Mary Magdalene."

My Thirst

My soul was thirsty for water,
That only the Savior could give,
The world had nothing to offer,
His water, I needed to live.

I tried all the things the world offered,
But nothing could help fill my heart,
I longed for something that mattered,
With Jesus, I got a new start.

If your soul's feeling empty and lonely,
Just open the door of your heart,
He'll then take your hand and will hold you,
And His love to you, He'll impart.

If it's peace and comfort you're craving,
Your Savior, He wants to be,
Just call on His name, in earnest,
A change in your life you will see.

Author: Betty H. Caldwell

John 4:14 "But whosoever drinketh of the water that I shall give him shall never thirst . . ."

No Second Chance

For those of you with troubles,
Just rest in Jesus' love,
You'll see Him with the angels,
Revealed from up above.

He'll set His feet on Olivet,
Your foes, He won't deliver,
Destruction is their new apparel,
Their death will make you shiver.

There'll be no second chances,
For those who were deceived,
They had their chance on Earth to pray,
But never would believe.

It's not too late to trust Him,
Repent, new life He'll give,
Just let the Master save you,
Eternal life, you'll live.

Author: Betty H. Caldwell

Hebrews 9:97 "And as it is appointed unto men once to die, but after this the judgment: . . ."

Second Birth

When a baby comes into the world,
We celebrate its birth,
Our hearts are filled with gladness,
With joy and with mirth.

Its little face brings happiness,
As we plan its life ahead,
We know not what tomorrow brings,
As we place it in its bed.

Our Father has great joy too,
And a band of angels sing,
Each time someone is born again,
The heavenly bells all ring.

We too are like that newborn babe,
When we are born again,
All Heaven celebrates with Him,
As we put away our sin.

Author: Betty H. Caldwell

John 3:3 "Jesus answered and said unto him, Verily, verily, I say unto thee, except a man be born again, he cannot see the kingdom of God."

The Bible

I found a book all dusty and worn,
Its cover was tattered and its pages were torn,
Some of the Words were written in red,
I then picked it up just to see what it said.

I opened it up with curious eyes,
And started to read, each day, line by line,
I found I was lost and undone in my ways,
But Christ, my Redeemer, forgave me one day.

I gave Him my life and obedience too,
He gave me assurance that all would be new,
The old man had died and a new one reborn,
I knew in my heart my troubles were few.

If you have a Bible that's still on the shelf,
Just open its cover and read for yourself,
When you do, you will learn He can save you today,
Just trust in His Word and obey, don't delay.

Author: Betty H. Caldwell

John 1: 12 "But as many as received him, to them gave he power to become the sons of God, even to them that believe on his name."

The Bridge

Sometimes in life we need a bridge,
To keep us safe and dry,
They take us where we want to go,
We never question why.

The old time saints had no such bridge,
Until our Savior came,
He carried them from Paradise,
To Heaven where He reigns.

When Jesus came and gave His life,
A bridge He made for us,
To carry us to Heaven's gates,
If we will only trust.

His bridge has spanned the centuries,
It's never very wide,
Just give your life to Him today,
He'll keep you by His side.

Author: Betty H Caldwell

John 14:6 "Jesus saith unto him, I am the way, the truth, and the life.
No one comes to the Father except through me."

The Garden of Eden

The Father made a perfect world,
In Eden on that day,
He only wanted fellowship,
But sin got in the way.

God gave them all they'd ever need,
The sun and moon for light,
He gave them food and shelter,
And kept them in His Sight.

Fellowship with God was not,
Enough for Eve and Adam,
They tasted God's forbidden fruit,
They thought it wouldn't matter.

God knew that He must save them,
And cleanse them come what may,
A sacrifice was needed,
Blood was the only way.

Author: Betty H. Caldwell

Genesis 2:8 "And the Lord planted a garden eastward in Eden; and there he put the man whom he had formed."

Whispers

God whispers in the gentle breeze,
And in the leaves that fall,
He whispers in the ocean waves,
And in the mountains tall.

He whispers in the evening,
And in the morning rain,
As birds begin their melodies,
That cause my heart to sing.

If only all could know my Lord,
And see just what I see,
The world would be a better place,
For each of you and me.

He whispers in your heart each day,
Don't tell Him to go away,
Invite Him in to visit you,
And in your heart, He'll stay.

Author: Betty H. Caldwell

Psalm 19: 1-2 "The heavens are telling of the glory of God; and their expanse is declaring the work of His hands."

Your Greatest Choice

A rose once grew between two thorns,
It struggled day-by-day,
The thorns tried hard to strangle it,
But it just grew and stayed.

It soon grew taller than the thorns,
With sun and rain each day,
The wind would blow and it would bend,
But steady, it would stay.

Our Savior hung between two thieves,
To Jesus, one would cling,
The other thief would not confess,
That Jesus Christ was King.

One man went to paradise,
The other one chose not to,
The choice that you can make today,
Will give a new life to you.

Author: Betty H. Caldwell

1 John 1:9 "If we confess our sins, he is faithful and just to forgive us our sins and to cleanse us from all unrighteousness."

Give Thanks

Thanksgiving Day is coming soon,
The preparation's great,
We hurry and we scurry,
And hope that we're not late.

The bird is browning nicely,
The stuffing's on the way,
And sweet aromas fill the air,
Let's feast without delay!

But wait, have we forgotten,
While everyone's in place,
The most important thing of all,
To bow our heads in grace.

You see, He feeds us daily,
If we would just receive,
His blessings are so many,
Just thank Him, and believe.

Author: Betty H. Caldwell

Psalm 100:4 "Enter into his gates with thanksgiving, and into his courts with praise: be thankful unto him and bless his name."

Honoring Christ

Did you honor Christ today?
Did you thank Him for His love?
What about the many blessings,
He sent you from above?

Sometimes we take for granted,
And push all thoughts aside,
Pretending we don't need our Lord,
With all our foolish pride.

I pray that you'll remember,
It was for you, He died,
He bore such pain and suffering,
As He was crucified.

He rose again in victory,
To save you from your sins,
Death and the grave were conquered,
Eternal life to win.

Author: Betty H. Caldwell

1 Corinthians 6:20 "For ye are bought with a price: therefore glorify God in your body and in your spirit which are God's."

Hummingbirds and Posies

The hummingbird is still with me,
Its presence I can see,
It's been my friend all summer long,
But soon, I know he'll flee.

His ruby throat shines in the sun,
He's such a sight to see,
Quickly sipping at each flower,
What joy for you and me.

He'll leave again and make his way,
To warmer winds and showers,
But he'll return again next spring,
To sip from all my flowers.

I thank You, Lord, for gracing me,
With hummingbirds and posies,
You thought of everything, it seems,
Like little birds and roses.

Author: Betty H. Caldwell

Song of Solomon 2: 12 "The flowers appear on the earth; the time of the singing of birds is come, and the voice of the turtle is heard in our land."

My Needs

I've never asked for silver,
And I don't ask for gold,
No earthly treasures either,
No riches so untold.

I only ask that You Lord,
Meet meager needs, that's all,
Please keep me in Your presence,
And help me when I fall.

You give me strength when I am weak,
You keep me safe from harm,
You bear me up on eagle's wings,
I have no fear at all.

So what else could I ask for,
You give me all I need,
Without You in my life, Lord,
No telling where I'd be.

Author: Betty H. Caldwell

Philippians 4: 19 "But my God shall supply all your need according to his riches in glory by Jesus Christ."

Thankful

I am so thankful, Lord,
That You have heard my plea,
Sometimes when I am weak,
Your strength still carries me.

Though Satan causes doubt,
And often brings me fear,
I call upon Your Holy Name,
And they all disappear.

The shelter of Your arms,
Is where I want to be,
So wrap me in Your precious love,
Far from the stormy sea.

So Lord, just let me always,
Rely on You alone,
Remove all fear and doubt from me,
And always keep me strong.

Author: Betty H. Caldwell

Ephesians 5:20 "Giving thanks always for all things unto God and the Father in the name of our Lord, Jesus Christ."

Thank You for the Rain

It's raining in my life these days,
It just won't go away,
It seems that when one trial's resolved,
Another comes to stay.

God says it rains on all of us,
The unjust and the just,
But Lord, I'm slowly drowning,
Please help me, Lord, you must.

I know that You'll be with me,
Through all my toils and strife,
You said, I'll never be alone,
With You first in my life.

So Lord, just take and use me,
I'll try not to complain,
I'll thank you for the sunshine,
And praise You for the rain.

Author: Betty H. Caldwell

1 Peter 5: 10 "But the God of all grace who hath called us unto his eternal glory by Christ Jesus, after that ye have suffered a while, make you perfect, . . ."

Waiting for Him

I just want to worship You,
And feel Your power flow,
With peace that only You can give,
I'll follow where You go.

I just want to do Your Will,
Your Spirit's in my soul,
The world has nothing for me here,
My life's in Your control.

I want to thank you, Lord,
For the cross and Calvary,
And for the blood You shed for me,
And death upon the tree.

When You return again one day,
Your children to receive,
The world will see You as You are,
For Satan can't deceive.

Author: Betty H. Caldwell

1 John 3:2 " . . . and it doth not yet appear what we shall be: but we know
that, when he shall appear, we shall be like him; for we shall see him as he is. "

Walking With Jesus

As I walk in the cool of the morning,
The wind gently tugs at my sleeve,
The leaves are spiraling downward,
They're hiding a deer, I believe.

The stillness is oh, so peaceful,
I could stay on this path all the day,
Forgetting the stress of my troubles,
In my heart, I am humming away.

My heart is full of His comfort,
Sweet peace only God can restore,
The joy of knowing my Savior,
I long just to know Him some more.

His peace can be yours for the asking,
Your life can be worth so much more,
A friendship you'll find, like no other,
If you'll only open the door.

Author: Betty H. Caldwell

Psalm 16:11 "Thou wilt show me the path of life; in thy presence is fullness of joy; at thy right hand there are pleasures for evermore."

Wonderful Grace

What would we do if not for grace,
And got just what we earned?
What if He showed no mercy,
Or never was concerned?

For all of us are sinners,
And some are saved by grace,
But what if God turned us away,
To never see His Face?

Then we'd be lost forever,
No hope to live again,
No chance for life eternal,
Just punishment for sin.

I thank Him for His mercy,
For grace and all He's done,
Salvation has been paid in full,
By Christ, God's Only Son.

Author: Betty H. Caldwell

Ephesians 4:7 "But to each one of us grace has been given as Christ apportioned it."

Cast Your Care

If you are feeling anxious,
As you lay your head to rest,
Cast all your cares upon Him,
For He will always bless.

The troubled times we live in,
Can sometimes bring despair,
But He knows all our troubles,
And the number of our hairs.

Although sometimes we feel alone,
And sometimes we can't see,
But God can still be with us,
If we'll just let Him be.

Our Lord will never fail us,
He said He'd never leave,
I'll love my Lord forever,
In Him I will believe.

Author: Betty H. Caldwell

1 Peter 5:7 "Casting all your care upon him; for he careth for you."

Dark Valleys

Sometimes the valleys are so deep,
That we can hardly see,
Above the mountains tall and steep,
And does He hear our plea?

But we must still remember,
The valleys make us strong,
If we stayed on the mountain,
Our strength would suffer long.

When we walk through dark valleys,
Our Lord is walking too,
He'll stay with us through trouble,
Our strength, He will renew.

He'll even carry you,
When you are overwhelmed,
He'll gladly take your burdens,
Just put your trust in Him.

Author: Betty H. Caldwell

Psalm 55:22 "Cast thy burden upon the Lord, and he shall sustain thee;
he shall never suffer the righteous to be moved."

Rainbows

A rainbow is God's promise,
His scriptures tell us so,
The splendor of its beauty,
Is something to behold.

His covenant is with us,
He said He'd never leave,
Just take His Hand and trust Him,
His blessings you'll receive.

In trouble, trial, and heartache,
We think we are alone,
But God is still in Glory,
And reigns upon His throne.

So take Him at His promise,
He'll always be with you,
He'll share your trials and troubles,
And bring you safely through.

Author: Betty H. Caldwell

Genesis 9: 13 "I do set my bow in the cloud, and it shall be for a token of a covenant between me and the earth."

Solitude

The early morn brings solitude,
And peace within my soul,
The waking of God's morning,
Is something to behold.

The melody of songbirds,
Brings sweetness to the air,
They know He'll always feed them,
And keep them in His care.

He cares for all that He has made,
His Word tells us it's true,
He knows each time a sparrow falls,
And also cares for you.

If you will only trust Him,
When life brings you distress,
He'll hold you close in comfort,
And you, He'll truly bless.

Author: Betty H. Caldwell

Matthew 6:6 "But thou, when thou prayest, enter into thy closet, and when thou hast shut the door, pray to the Father which is in secret; and thy Father . . . "

Total Surrender

It's hard to show just how we feel,
To loved ones and to friends,
We think we may look foolish,
So sometimes, we pretend.

We may fool friends and loved ones,
But God is not a fool,
He knows what you are thinking,
And what you say and do.

With Him, you must surrender,
Your thoughts and feelings too,
It shows you truly trust Him,
And that your love is true.

So give your total self to God,
His blessings to receive,
Just start by falling on your knees,
Repent, and then believe.

Author: Betty H. Caldwell

Psalm 112:7 "He shall not be afraid of evil tidings: his heart is fixed, trusting in the Lord."

Your Vessel

So many times we struggle,
To hold Your Hand, it seems,
Sometimes, we fail to look to You,
When it's You we really need.

I'm just a lowly piece of clay,
For You to mold and make,
A useful vessel for Your Will,
If only I obey.

So chip the edges from me,
To live a life that's true,
Polish, Lord, and change my heart,
To make me more like You.

Someday, I may feel worthy,
To say I am Your child,
When I become a vessel,
Without my worldly pride.

Author: Betty H. Caldwell

Isaiah 64:8 "But now, O Lord, you are our Father; we are the clay, and you are our potter; we are all the work of your hand."

Jesus Christ FOREVER

Inspirational Poetry To Live By

God has blessed me with a love for creativity. My hobbies include oil and acrylic painting of landscapes and wildlife, gardening, and writing Christian poetry. I am a wife, mother of two sons, and the grandmother of four beautiful grandchildren. God has truly blessed me with a wonderful family.

In my professional career, I was a management analyst for the United States Army at Fort Monroe, Virginia. Writing assignments were a significant part of my job. After several years of retirement, I began to miss the connection with others provided by writing. God has now opened this door allowing me an opportunity to tell others about Him through my poetry. For this blessing, I am truly grateful to my Savior, Jesus Christ.

JESUS CHRIST – FOREVER is my way of reaching out to the lost and providing comfort to Christians who are struggling with everyday problems.

— Betty H. Caldwell

CPSIA information can be obtained
at www.ICGtesting.com
Printed in the USA
FFOW04n1435230216
21749FF